Belongs to .

____

Things to remember

You don't have to be perfect

Having a bad day is okay

Small steps are also progress

Asking for help is strength

People love and appreciate you

[illegible]

[illegible]